COLOR, CULTURE, & CREED
How Ethnic Background Influences Belief

RELIGION & MODERN CULTURE
Title List

COLOR, CULTURE, & CREED
How Ethnic Background Influences Belief

by Kenneth McIntosh, M.Div.,
and Marsha McIntosh

Mason Crest Publishers
Philadelphia

Mason Crest Publishers Inc.
370 Reed Road
Broomall, Pennsylvania 19008
(866) MCP-BOOK (toll free)

First printing
1 2 3 4 5 6 7 8 9 10

Library of Congress Cataloging-in-Publication Data

McIntosh, Kenneth, 1959–
   Color, culture & creed : how ethnic background influences belief /
by Kenneth R. McIntosh and Marsha L. McIntosh.
      p. cm. — (Religion and modern culture)
   Includes bibliographical references and index.
   ISBN 1-59084-976-0 ISBN 1-59084-970-1 (series)
   1. Christianity and culture. 2. Ethnicity—Religious aspects
—Christianity. 3. Faith. 4. Belief and doubt.   I. McIntosh, Marsha.
II. Title. III. Title: Color, culture, and creed. IV. Series.
BR115.C8M263 2006
200'.89—dc22

Produced by Harding House Publishing Service, Inc.
www.hardinghousepages.com
Interior design by Dianne Hodack.
Cover design by MK Bassett-Harvey.
Printed in India.

CONTENTS

INTRODUCTION

by Dr. Marcus J. Borg

You are about to begin an important and exciting experience: the study of modern religion. Knowing about religion—and religions—is vital for understanding our neighbors, whether they live down the street or across the globe.

Despite the modern trend toward religious doubt, most of the world's population continues to be religious. Of the approximately six billion people alive today, around two billion are Christians, one billion are Muslims, 800 million are Hindus, and 400 million are Buddhists. Smaller numbers are Sikhs, Shinto, Confucian, Taoist, Jewish, and indigenous religions.

Religion plays an especially important role in North America. The United States is the most religious country in the Western world: about 80 percent of Americans say that religion is "important" or "very important" to them. Around 95 percent say they believe in God. These figures are very different in Europe, where the percentages are much smaller. Canada is "in between": the figures are lower than for the United States, but significantly higher than in Europe. In Canada, 68 percent of citizens say religion is of "high importance," and 81 percent believe in God or a higher being.

The United States is largely Christian. Around 80 percent describe themselves as Christian. In Canada, professing Christians are 77 percent of the population. But religious diversity is growing. According to Harvard scholar Diana Eck's recent book *A New Religious America*, the United States has recently become the most religiously diverse country in the world. Canada is also a country of great religious variety.

Fifty years ago, religious diversity in the United States meant Protestants, Catholics, and Jews, but since the 1960s, immigration from Asia, the Middle East, and Africa has dramatically increased the number of people practicing other religions. There are now about six million Muslims, four million Buddhists, and a million Hindus in the United States. To compare these figures to two historically important Protestant denominations in the United States, about 3.5 million are Presbyterians and 2.5 million are Episcopalians. There are more Buddhists in the United States than either of these denominations, and as many Muslims as the two denominations combined. This means that knowing about other religions is not just knowing about people in other parts of the world—but about knowing people in our schools, workplaces, and neighborhoods.

Moreover, religious diversity does not simply exist between religions. It is found within Christianity itself:

• There are many different forms of Christian worship. They range from Quaker silence to contemporary worship with rock music to traditional liturgical worship among Catholics and Episcopalians to Pentecostal enthusiasm and speaking in tongues.

- Christians are divided about the importance of an afterlife. For some, the next life—a paradise beyond death—is their primary motive for being Christian. For other Christians, the afterlife does not matter nearly as much. Instead, a relationship with God that transforms our lives this side of death is the primary motive.
- Christians are divided about the Bible. Some are biblical literalists who believe that the Bible is to be interpreted literally and factually as the inerrant revelation of God, true in every respect and true for all time. Other Christians understand the Bible more symbolically as the witness of two ancient communities—biblical Israel and early Christianity—to their life with God.

Christians are also divided about the role of religion in public life. Some understand "separation of church and state" to mean "separation of religion and politics." Other Christians seek to bring Christian values into public life. Some (commonly called "the Christian Right") are concerned with public policy issues such as abortion, prayer in schools, marriage as only heterosexual, and pornography. Still other Christians name the central public policy issues as American imperialism, war, economic injustice, racism, health care, and so forth. For the first group, values are primarily concerned with individual behavior. For the second group, values are also concerned with group behavior and social systems. The study of religion in North America involves not only becoming aware of other religions but also becoming aware of differences within Christianity itself. Such study can help us to understand people with different convictions and practices.

And there is one more reason why such study is important and exciting: religions deal with the largest questions of life. These questions are intellectual, moral, and personal. Most centrally, they are:

- What is real? The religions of the world agree that "the real" is more than the space-time world of matter and energy.
- How then shall we live?
- How can we be "in touch" with "the real"? How can we connect with it and become more deeply centered in it?

This series will put you in touch with other ways of seeing reality and how to live.

Chapter 1

THE SPIRITS
OF OUR ANCESTORS

"Hinduism is rambunctious, open, public, full of festivals and free of guilt. For many, it is above all a religion grounded in community." That is how writer Shoba Narayan describes the religion of her childhood in India, in an article posted on Belief.net. She recalls Hindu festivals that were "spectacles of light and color" with firecrackers and floats.

When Shoba recalls her childhood in India, where Hindu belief is part of everyday culture, she wonders, "How, then, was I going to raise my daughter as a Hindu in a Christian country?" She reflects on the route taken by some of her Indian friends: "They name their children Neil or Megan, ignore their Hindu roots, and celebrate Christmas. It is easier on the kids, they say." But Shoba refuses to go that route.

Hinduism has been an anchor in her life—an anchor she wants her children to know also. As she admits, "Deciding to raise my daughter as a Hindu was the easy part. Actually doing it will be the hard part." Shoba arranged for five other Hindu families to meet together for a monthly potluck, sing Hindu songs, and discuss their faith. She got books about the gods and goddesses to read to her daughter at night.

Raising her daughter with Indian beliefs in the United States isn't easy. Shoba says, "She loves wearing Indian clothes, but she doesn't know any Hindu festivals. Firecrackers are illegal in America, and building a life-size image of the goddess Kali is simply not possible in our tiny New York apartment." When Shoba tried to play tapes of *Sanskrit* chants in the morning, her daughter protested that she wanted to watch *Barney* and *Teletubbies*. At night, her daughter prefers to sing "Twinkle, Twinkle, Little Star" rather than "Hare Rama." Nonetheless, Shoba persists. She says, "One measure of comfort is the realization that thousands of Hindus in America are treading on that path along with me." Shoba Narayan values the religious traditions connected to her cultural background.

COLOR, CULTURE, & CREED CONNECT

What makes someone a Buddhist or a Muslim or a Christian or a Jew? Is it just a matter of personal choice? Do people receive their religious beliefs from their families—or from their national backgrounds? How much does the culture a person was born into determine spiritual beliefs?

This book explores the ways that cultural backgrounds influence religious belief. Race, tribe, and language all combine to give each person his or her sense of identity. Along with color and culture comes religious heritage. In the United States and Canada, some people come

GLOSSARY

evangelical: Relating to a Protestant Christian church whose members believe in the authority of the Bible and salvation through the acceptance of Jesus Christ as one's personal savior.

First Nations: The groups of people who lived first in the Americas, before the coming of Europeans; a Canadian term for the people Americans often refer to as Native Americans.

generalizations: Wide-based and sweeping conclusions based on information that may be unique to a particular individual or situation.

Sanskrit: An ancient language that is the classical language of India and Hinduism.

stereotypes: Mental pictures that apply overly simplified or prejudiced characteristics to any individual that belongs to a particular group.

from families who have been here for generations; others are recent immigrants. Different religious traditions are maintained within various ethnic backgrounds.

Many North Americans, especially those of European ancestry, view religious faith as an entirely personal choice. Citizens of the United States and Canada are used to the separation of church and state. Many families grow up with little religiosity, and even in religious homes, some parents feel it is valuable to "let the children choose their own religion."

This contrasts with nations where culture, race, and religion are connected. Around the world, innumerable people believe their ethnic, cultural, and religious practices are inseparable. Entire tribes, villages, and even nations celebrate religious festivals together, recite the same prayers in schools and businesses, and allow their government, village elders, or other leaders to make decisions based on religious beliefs. Immigrants from such cultures may assume, "I am a Buddhist/ Muslim/Hindu because my family/village/national heritage is that religion."

Within the United States and Canada, some cultural groups have a strong sense of religious identity tied to their ethnicity. Until recently, most Italian Americans, Irish Americans, and French Canadians regarded the Roman Catholic faith as an essential part of their identity. Latinos have also traditionally been devout in their Catholic belief.

Among many minority groups, religion has played a vital role in cultural survival. For centuries, the church has sustained black communities, providing hope in the face of prejudice and performing practical services that white society denied them. The black church continues to be a vital force in African American neighborhoods. At the same time, many blacks have embraced Islam as a genuinely African religion.

Realizing the connection between religious and cultural survival, Europeans in the United States and Canada attempted for five centuries to demolish Native religions. Despite the outlawing of important traditional ceremonies and attempts to eradicate their spirituality, many *First Nations* people continue to worship in the ways of their ancient ancestors. Today, traditional spirituality often plays a vital role in Native self-identity.

Recent immigrants to the United States and Canada often come from countries that do not separate religion and culture. Indian Hindus, Muslims from Indonesia and Pakistan, Copts from Egypt, Buddhists from Laos and Tibet, and others bring with them the belief that their religion is part of their culture and personal identity.

RELIGION & MODERN CULTURE

THE VOICE OF YOUR ANCESTORS

Popular Vietnamese Buddhist teacher Thich Nhat Hanh emphasizes the need for every believer—of any faith—to "listen to the voice of your spiritual ancestors." He believes this is a valuable reason to stay with the faith of one's ancestors, whatever that faith might be. Hanh urges Christians to "be the best Christian you can be" rather than convert to his own Buddhist faith.

FAITH OF OUR FATHERS?

Billy Graham is probably the most influential American religious figure in recent history. The famous *evangelical* preacher is fond of saying, "God has no grandchildren!" By this, Graham means that each person must choose for or against God; he does not believe that faith can be passed down from generation to generation. The evangelist often states that one is not a Christian simply because she is born to a Christian family or in a Christian country. Instead, Graham affirms, each person must have a personal relationship with God.

Billy Graham's statement reflects modern North American culture, which emphasizes personal freedom. Members of most Anglo-American families feel free to make important decisions—whom to marry, whether to take a job, where to attend church—without consulting parents or other relatives. By contrast, families of Asian or Middle Eastern background function more as units. Even adult children make important decisions together with their parents and extended family. In ethnic and cultural groups that emphasize family, clan, or tribe, the group rather than the individual makes religious decisions. For a traditional Hindu family, Billy Graham's statement would seem absurd. They might think, "What does he mean? God has plenty of grandchildren—look at our family!"

Cultures that emphasize family duty and togetherness also often place a strong emphasis on the role of ancestors in one's religious life. For Latino families, the tie between living and dead is especially strong on *Dia de los Muertos* (Day of the Dead). Many Pueblo Indians in the southwestern United States leave corn offerings on the table at every meal, reminders that the spirits of the ancestors are still present with the living. Asian cultures and religions honor ancestors as well.

CULTURE & RELIGIOUS CHOICES

The United States and Canada are the most religiously diverse nations in the world. This great variety of religious belief can present a wonderful opportunity to learn, yet it can also challenge people's beliefs. Immigrants from Asian and Middle Eastern countries often struggle raising children with the religious beliefs of their homeland in a country that has very different values. In Canada, many people feel that religion is simply unimportant for modern society. Such sentiments are threatening for members of cultures built on religious beliefs that have endured for thousands of years. Many believers feel threatened and anxious when their traditional ways face a new culture.

For example, when Rahul Kohli and Sultana Iqbal said, "I do," at the altar, they also said, "I don't," to family members who wanted them to

RELIGION & MODERN CULTURE

follow religious tradition and deny their love for one another. According to an article on the Little India Web site:

> Rahul married his college sweetheart, who happened to be Muslim. "Marrying Sultana was the biggest battle of my life," Rahul says, adding that his parents felt completely let down by his choice. Until the day of the move, he was receiving hysterical phone calls from relatives back in India, imploring him not to leave his parents!

Friends of the family cut off relationships with the elder Kohlis—even though they opposed their son's marriage—because the family now had a Muslim member.

Religious choices are complex. They can bring great happiness, but sometimes they can be very painful. What factors led you to make the spiritual decisions that have shaped your life? Was it mostly your own personal choice—or have your ethnic identity, family, or cultural heritage shaped your spiritual beliefs? For most people, a combination of factors influences religious decisions. Personal religious choices are rarely free from cultural and social circumstances.

As you read this book, try not to develop *stereotypes* based on the information you encounter. This book contains generalizations. While these *generalizations* are factual regarding groups or movements, they may not be true regarding specific individuals. Each person is unique. Your Canadian and U.S. neighbors are amazingly diverse and creative—so don't make assumptions about someone you know. If you want to know what she believes or where he worships, ask! Just remember to do so politely.

Chapter 2

NATIVE SPIRITUALITY— HONORING MOTHER EARTH

"Who are you?" the petite Vietnamese woman asked.

"Mike," the American soldier responded.

"No, who *are* you?" she insisted with intense curiosity in her voice.

Mike gave his name and troop number this time.

Unsatisfied, the woman asked one more time, "No, *who are you*?" The Vietnamese woman then explained. She had learned about the **indigenous** peoples of the Earth. Mike looked like a Native American, and she wanted to know who he was.

Mike understood now. "I'm Mike of the Mohawk tribe."

A smile spread across the woman's face. "Ah, your people are like my people." They went on to discuss the similarities of their tribes. The next day the woman returned. "Our family invites you to live in our longhouse. We want you to be one of us while you are in Vietnam."

Today, Mike has tears in his eyes when he describes the care the Vietnamese people showed him during the rest of his duty in Vietnam. Mike's time there helped him connect with his own Native culture. It also left him emotionally wounded—but when he went home, he found healing through the spiritual traditions of his Mohawk heritage.

Today, many Native American people are reconnecting with their spiritual and traditional roots. For these men and women of the First Nations, the question, "Who are you?" connects with, "What do you believe?"

NATIVE SPIRITUALITY TIED TO THE LAND

Most historians estimate 50,000,000 people lived in the Americas in 1492. Though European explorers found this land rich with natural resources, they did not grasp the cultural and spiritual wealth of the land's Native people.

Many indigenous people regard their land as given to them by the Creator. The Zuni are one example. Zuni believe they emerged into the daylight world from the underneath world at Ribbon Falls, in the Grand Canyon, where their Twin War Gods led them onto the earth's surface. A brightly colored parrot led part of the group to what is now Mexico and Central America, and a crow led the others to the Middle Place, Halona, New Mexico, today known as Zuni.

All First Nations groups feel connected to the lands they come from. Their cultural sense of self weaves together land, spiritual practice, and political defense of the land. As a result, many tribes are working to reclaim their ancestral territories. For example, Winona LaDuke, a member of the Mississippi Band, White Earth Anishinabe (Ojibwa), has distinguished herself for her environmental and political work, including a run for vice president of the United States in the year 2000. LaDuke is founder of the White Earth Land Recovery Project (WELRP), whose focus is to raise funds to buy back lands previously owned by the White Earth people. The organization's dream is to own enough land to grow herbs and plants for medicines and to sustain traditional harvesters and craftspeople.

NATIVE DEMOGRAPHICS

In July of 2002, the U.S. Census estimated that 4.3 million Native Americans and Alaskan Natives lived in the United States. The most populous Indian nation in the United States is the Navajo with 175,200 tribal members. Most Native people lived in rural areas until the 1960s. As of 2002, however, 66 percent lived in urban areas. This is the lowest urban percentage of any racial group.

"Life is not separate from death. It only looks that way."

—*Blackfoot proverb*

The 2001 data from Statistics Canada records approximately one million **Aboriginals**. Of these, 49 percent live in urban areas. The province with the highest numbers of First Nations members is Ontario, with 141,520 recorded in the 1996 census.

THE IMPORTANCE OF NATIVE FAITH

The arrival of Europeans brought great changes to the culture of Native Americans and the Aboriginal people of Canada. Yet traditional spirituality and culture have endured through all the changes, and they continue to be important to many Indians and First Nations peoples.

In the Navajo language, there is no word for religion. A tribal member considers livestock, his home, his fields, the sky, and the ground where he walks as sacred. The Navajo see spirituality in every aspect of life around them. Because of this, spirituality defines Indian identity as much as blood and lifestyle do.

Native spirituality is also important for conveying a sense of self-identity and place in the world. For an Apache girl, for instance, the Sunrise Dance, or the "Changing Woman Ceremony," marks the change from childhood to womanhood. Approximately one in three Apache girls has a Sunrise Dance. During the days of songs, dances, and prayers, a medicine man oversees the ceremony. The whole experience brings the community closer as together they worship, pray, and give and receive gifts. Apache women who have experienced this ceremony talk about how it gave them a new sense of spiritual power. The ceremony is becoming popular once more with adolescent girls because it

"The American Indian is of the soil, whether it be the region of the forests, plains, pueblos, or mesas. He fits into the landscape, for the land that fashioned the continent also fashioned the man for his surroundings. He once grew as naturally as the sunflowers; he belongs just as the buffalo belongs."

—*Luther Standing Bear (1868?–1939), Oglala Sioux Chief*

gives them a sense of dignity and importance in the community at a time when many Indian teen girls lack a sense of their place in the world. The Changing Woman Ceremony strengthens their sense of self-identity as young Native women.

One Native woman found strength to overcome adversity from a traditional tribal lore. Lori Arviso Alvord tells her story in her autobiography, *The Scalpel and the Silver Bear.* Lori grew up on the Navajo Reservation, and life was not easy for her. Her father was Navajo but her mother was blond-haired and blue-eyed. Lori had a difficult time finding her place in the world. A traditional story of a woman whose husband died at the hands of enemies particularly impressed her, however; with the help of Coyote, the woman turned into a savage bear and killed her husband's murderers. Coming from the bear clan, this story had special meaning for Lori. She imagined herself having the strength of the bear. The story gave her the courage to overcome adversity and follow her dream to become the first Navajo female surgeon. Her spiritual belief provided a powerful sense of self, and she was able to achieve much in her life in spite of cultural barriers to success.

BISON & PEOPLE SURVIVE TOGETHER

The Crow tribe purchased a herd of 400 bison in 1971. They now have the largest herd in Indian country at over 1,500 head. Bison are still spiritually and culturally important to the Plains Indian Nations. Like the bison, Plains Indian culture was targeted for extermination, and, like the bison, it has survived and is growing stronger.

THE GENOCIDE & SUPPRESSION OF NATIVE FAITHS

Millions of Aboriginal peoples died from illnesses and wars after the Europeans came. The governments of Canada and the United States forced Native populations off their lands. These governments also issued policies encouraging Native *assimilation* into white culture.

One way of forcing assimilation in both Canada and the United States was to remove Native children from their families and provide education for them in government boarding schools. Native spirituality was also restricted in both countries. Spiritual leaders faced years in jail if they practiced certain religious ceremonies.

In the United States, the Indian Removal Act of 1830 forced many Eastern tribes to leave their forested lands and live on barren plains. Daily life in these wooded regions had been the basis for Eastern tribes' cultural and spiritual beliefs and practices. Meanwhile, as European

NATIVE SPIRITUALITY—
HONORING MOTHER EARTH

"Because God loves all of us he put this medicine [peyote] in the world so that the Indians would find it and through it they would come to Christ."

—*Emerson Spider, head of the Native American Church in South Dakota*

newcomers hunted the bison (also called the American buffalo) to extinction, the Plains people of the Dakota, Nakota, and Lakota lost their main resource for survival. Moreover, many of their spiritual and cultural rituals and dances became meaningless without the bison.

SURVIVAL TECHNIQUES

As their environments changed, some Native people altered their belief systems. A number accepted Christianity. Some refused to give up their tribal identity and religious practices. Others reformed their traditional beliefs to fit their new situations.

Several religious movements came from the reshaping of Native belief. At a time of crisis for the Iroquois Nation, for example, a man named Handsome Lake emerged. Settlers overran their territory, European diseases were spreading among their people, and alcohol was taking its toll on their men. During a severe illness, Handsome Lake received a vision in which he saw that the Iroquois Nation was suffering because it had turned away from right living. Handsome Lake received instruction on how to teach his people. He first overcame his own alcohol addiction and went on to lead the six nations of the Iroquois, giving them new hope and strength. Many Iroquois today follow Handsome Lake's religion.

"Our land, our religion, and our life are one."
—*Hopi creed*

In 1890, a movement began among the Kiowa and Apache in Oklahoma; a large number of First Nations people still belong to this group. Today, members call it the Native American Church (NAC). This church combines Native traditional beliefs with Christianity. It emphasizes Indian pride, traditional ceremonies, and strong morals. Members of the church sometimes use a hallucinogen, peyote, to enhance their spiritual experience. The NAC is a "Pan-Indian" belief, uniting the faith of different Native groups, and it has helped many Native peoples resist assimilation into the broader culture.

Caucasians tried to strip Canadian and U.S. Native Americans of their traditional ways and beliefs. Drug and alcohol abuse, suicide, and spouse and child abuse all result from living in a world where traditional ways and beliefs are absent. Numerous Native men and women have been able to regain control of their lives, jobs, and families when they reconnected with spiritual traditions.

CHRISTIANITY ON THE RESERVATIONS

A teenager stood before a group of peers and told her story. She comes from a remote Inuit village 400 miles (644 kilometers) from the closest road. The village has the highest suicide rate in North America. Her life seemed hopeless to her, and she did not feel as though she had a reason to live until she experienced Christian conversion. Now, she is involved with a Christian organization called On Eagle's Wings, a group composed of teenagers from thirty tribes. They travel to reservations sharing their "hope stories"—stories of how they have moved from hopelessness to hope through knowing the Creator's son, Jesus Christ.

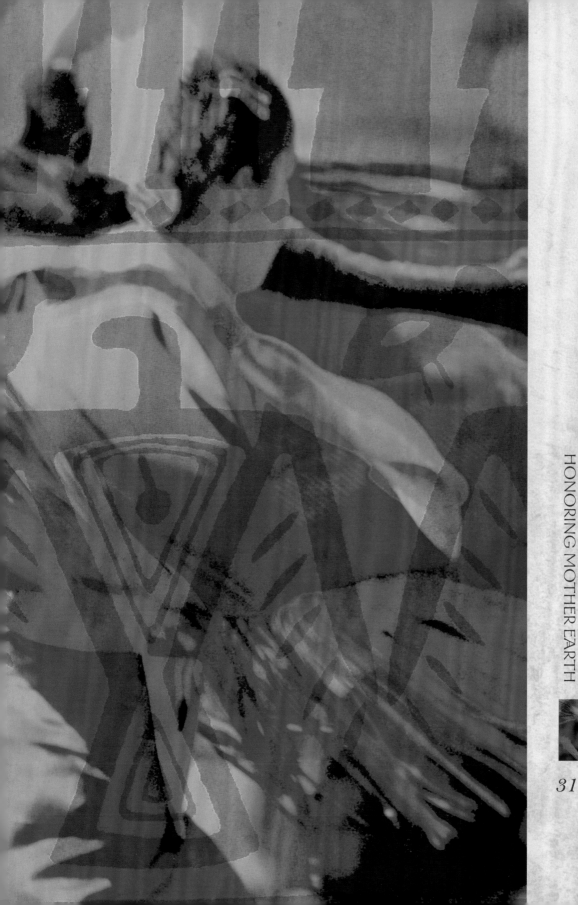

31

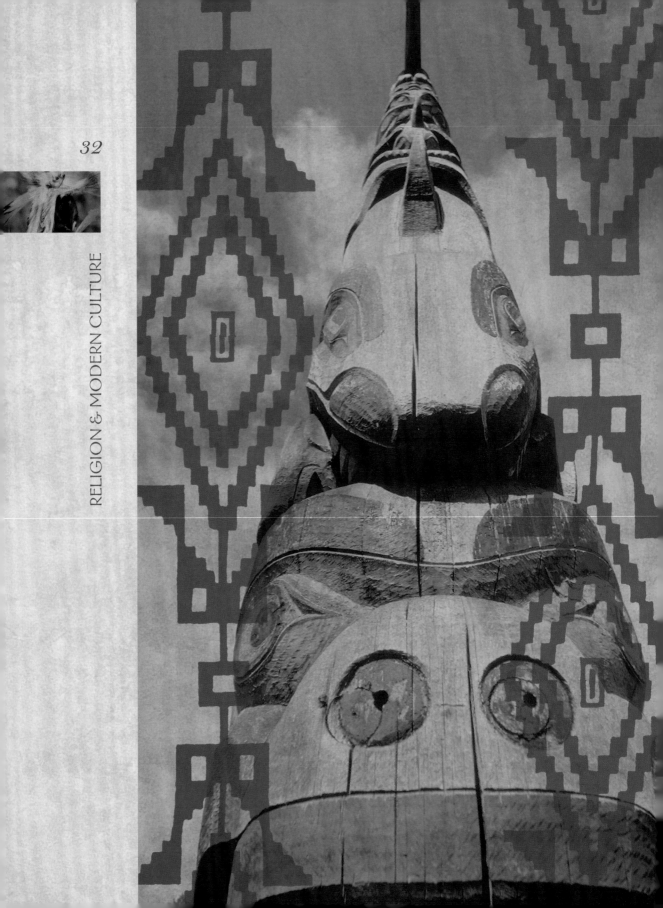

"Great Spirit! You lived first, and you are older than all need, older than all prayer. All things belong to you—the two-legged, the four-legged, the wings of the air and all green things that live."

—Black Elk, Oglala Sioux

Through the years, Native peoples have had three reactions to Christianity: rejection, a blending of Christianity with Native beliefs, and total acceptance. Tribal members who have left their traditional beliefs may still be very spiritual people. Some have rejected traditional practices. Others embrace aspects of their Native spirituality along with Christian faith. On most reservations, there is a variety of Christian churches.

THE REBIRTH OF NATIVE SPIRITUALITY TODAY

While some First Nations people find strength in Christianity, others believe that traditional spirituality is necessary for their personal and tribal survival. Karen Lonehill, the author of *North American Indians Today: Sioux*, says many families of the Lakota tribe have returned to practicing traditional ceremonies. More and more Native people are relying on traditional ways to find meaning and balance in their world today.

While Native people resisted European attacks on their culture, other minorities struggled for survival and equality. Slave traders brought Africans to work for colonists in the Caribbean, South America, and the United States. During centuries of mistreatment, Africans in the Americas found strength for survival in Christian, Muslim, and traditional African religions.

Chapter 3

RELIGION & MODERN CULTURE

AFRICAN HERITAGE

Prison inmates, barbers, a nightclub singer, several old-timer churchgoers, and a handful of rappers make up the black church choir that won the Gospel Explosion competition in the movie *The Fighting Temptations*. Cuba Gooding Jr. plays fast-talking New York City advertising executive Darrin Hill.

When Darrin's boss fires him, Darrin returns to his hometown in Georgia to attend his aunt's funeral. After the lawyer reads the will, Darrin learns his aunt left him a fortune—if he can fulfill her last wish: pull together a church choir and win the annual Gospel Explosion competition—and $150,000 will be his.

"Erase the white gods from your hearts. We must go back to our own native church to our own God."

—*George Alexander McGuire, founder of the African Orthodox Church*

Darrin, who begins as a dishonest, selfish, and rootless man, changes during the course of the movie. As he becomes involved in the black church and community, he reconnects with his heritage. The music and newfound relationships give Darrin a feeling of joy. When he tries to go back to his executive lifestyle, he misses the close connection he found at the church and is drawn back to stay. In the end, he knows he has found something much more valuable than an inheritance. He has found a community, love, and fulfillment.

Although the movie's story is fictional, for centuries, the church has been a real-life unifying force for blacks in the United States and Canada. It has been much more than a religious institution; it has been a lifeline for many members.

STATISTICS

According to the Barna Research Group, blacks are unusual among North American ethnic groups when it comes to spirituality. They live in the midst of a culture that has been relatively unsympathetic to their needs—but this experience has given them more openness to religion. Also according to Barna Research, blacks are more likely than other racial groups to live the teachings of Jesus, and they are more likely to say that the teachings of the Bible are accurate and that faith is very important to them. Their views of God are more apt to be traditional, and they believe they must spread their faith to others.

GLOSSARY

born-again Christians: Evangelical believers who indicate a definite point in time when they entered into a new life through the spiritual power of Jesus Christ.

camp meetings: Special religious gatherings that were usually held once a year outdoors, under arbors or tents.

pacifist: A person who does not believe in using violence to achieve goals, even during times of war.

pilgrimage: A journey made to a religious site for spiritual reasons.

prayer walks: Pleas for God's blessing on everything a person sees while walking around a particular area.

revivals: Times of spiritual renewal, often emotional, usually experienced by an entire community.

secular: Not controlled by a religious body or concerned with religious or spiritual matters.

Forty-seven percent of blacks say they are *born-again Christians*, whereas 41 percent of whites, 29 percent of Hispanics, and 12 percent of Asians call themselves born-again Christians. In a survey conducted in 2004, 91 percent of blacks said they prayed during the week, 59 percent read the Bible, 48 percent attended a religious service, and 57 percent strongly agreed that the Bible is accurate.

"There was preaching by the brothers, then praying and singing all around. The slave forgets all his sufferings except to remind others of the trials during the past week, exclaiming, 'Thank God we shall not live here always!'"

—Peter Randolph, slave

HISTORY OF THE BLACK CHURCH

Historians estimate Europeans brought nine and a half million slaves to the Caribbean and the Americas from the continent of Africa. Once the slaves arrived in the North American colonies, it did not take long for European settlers to rob them of their social ties and culture. Slave owners forbade the newcomers to use their languages. They split apart families. In fact, it was common for farm owners to buy and sell slaves just to break up families.

Despite slavery, the black church formed and grew. The message that a person could have a relationship with the Son of God was soothing and comforting to slaves. It provided a sense of worth and dignity. **Camp meetings** brought **revivals** that sometimes lasted for days. From these revivals came the most important parts of worship for the black church—music and storytelling. Music offered hope and encouragement to dreary lives. The slaves took church hymns and put different rhythms to them. They added chants, intonations, and made the music theirs. Storytelling is prominent in the African tradition, and preaching as storytelling was an important part of religion for blacks. The call-and-response method of preaching became a specialty of black preachers. Perhaps you have heard black church members call out "amen" or "all right" as they listen to their preachers. This is an aspect of call-and-response preaching.

HOW MANY BLACKS ARE THERE IN NORTH AMERICA?

In 2002, the U.S. Census showed there were 36 million blacks in the United States. In Canada, there were 662,200 blacks according to the 2001 census, making up 2.2 percent of the population. Much of Canada's black population lives on the East Coast. In Nova Scotia, 57 percent of the visible minorities are black, and on Prince Edward Island, 31 percent are black.

Slave owners forbade slaves from attending church services, but slaves held their own secret meetings. Somehow, they managed to meet, pray, preach, sing, and receive comfort and strength from these activities. Some have referred to the slave churches at this time as the "new invisible institution."

During the reconstruction time after the Civil War, black churches were the main sources of spiritual and material aid for blacks. They became the political, social, and cultural centers for black communities. Preachers helped give direction to families. They encouraged adults to build strong families and to be faithful to one spouse and their children. Because slave masters often separated families, slaves sometimes did not learn how to live as families. The church therefore became even more important as the foundation of the black family.

In the late 1800s, the U.S. government passed discriminatory laws that separated blacks from the rest of society. (These laws became

"As I reflect down the vistas of the past, as I think about the problems and experiences I have had; without a faith in God, a faith in prayer, and a disposition of loyalty to God, I don't know what I would have done."

—C. L. Franklin, *African American minister*

known as Jim Crow laws.) Blacks had to have separate schools, restaurants, and even drinking fountains. According to Norma Jean Lutz in *The History of the Black Church*, churches functioned as social-service centers that helped the black community in times of poverty, sickness, and death. They formed societies such as the Brothers and Sisters of Charity and Sons and Daughters of Esther. Later, some of these became *secular* insurance companies. Blacks also began to open banks. The dominant culture forced blacks into their own institutions. The church was one of those, and therefore, it became central to people's lives.

CHRISTIAN LEADERS IN THE CIVIL RIGHTS MOVEMENT

In the 1950s, American society began to change in an important way. On December 1, 1955, a quiet seamstress boarded a city bus in Montgomery, Alabama. She sat in the first row of the black section in the back of the bus. As the ride progressed, all the seats designated for whites filled up. When one more white man boarded, the bus driver ordered the seamstress, Rosa Parks, to move to the back and give up her seat. She refused and peacefully sat there. Soon the police arrived. They handcuffed her and took her to jail.

Ministers from black churches all over the city encouraged a boycott of the bus system, the first locally initiated protest against racial discrimination. This one event helped spark the civil rights movement in the United States. And during the bus boycott, a spiritual leader of the new movement came forward. Martin Luther King Jr. had just become the pastor of the Dexter Avenue Baptist church in Montgomery. He joined the boycott and went on to become a driving force behind the movement.

The civil rights movement of the 1950s and 1960s was born in black churches. A well-organized group emerged, made up of leaders who were, first of all, leaders in the church. This group was the Southern Christian Leadership Conference. Dr. King strove to use Christian principles in all actions of the movement. He also admired and followed the *pacifist* teachings of Hindu spiritual leader Mohandas Gandhi.

Leon Sullivan, the pastor of Zion Baptist Church in Philadelphia, was also a leader in the civil rights movement. He began a boycott of businesses engaged in selective patronage—in other words, they did not

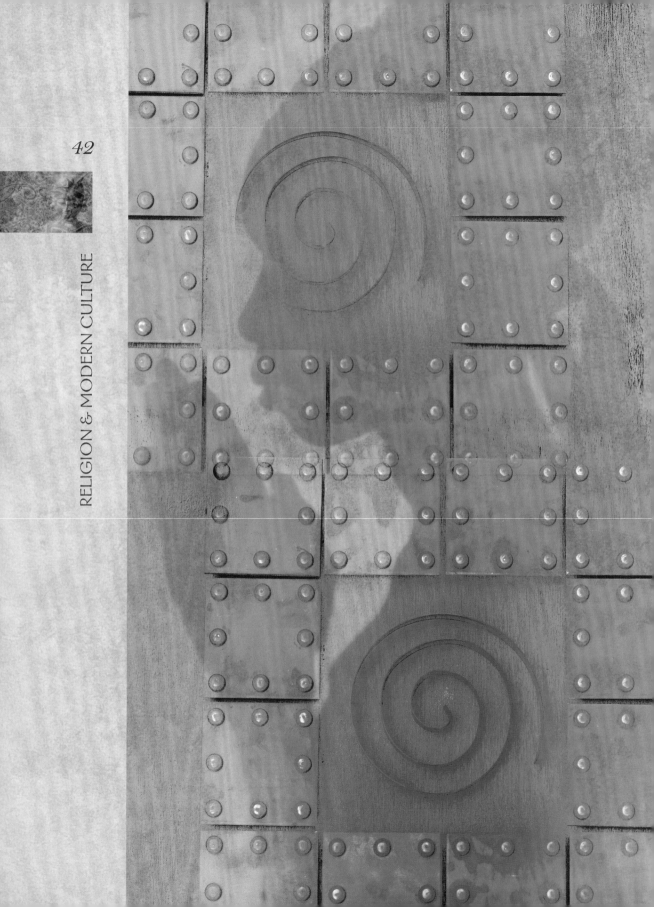

CANADIAN BLACK HISTORY

In 1826, the first black church in Toronto opened as part of the Underground Railroad. It supported antislavery activities, had antislavery bazaars, and hosted lectures. After the United States passed the Fugitive Slave Act in 1850, the government had the authority to catch runaway slaves and return them to their owners. Runaway slaves began to go to Canada to escape their slave masters. In 1851, there were thirty-four black business owners and tradespeople. By 1860, at least 1,500 citizens of Toronto were black.

employ enough blacks in their operations nor did they encourage blacks to do business there. He also opened schools called Opportunities Industrialization Centers. These schools trained African Americans to develop the skills they needed to be able to fill available jobs.

BLACK MUSLIMS

When slave traders brought West Africans to North America and the Caribbean, many of the slaves were Muslims. Slave masters did all they could to strip the slaves of their former cultures and religions. Some

"God is always capable of making something out of nothing."

—*Louis Farrakhan, Nation of Islam leader*

clung to them secretly. Because of this, a hundred years after gaining their freedom, their grandchildren were able to return to the faith of their ancestors.

In the 1930s, Nobel Drew Ali started the Moorish Science Temple of Islam. He used as his scripture the Holy Koran of the Moorish Science Temple of America, which differed from the Qur'an—the holy book recorded by Mohammad. Wallace D. Fard, and then Elijah Muhammad, led the Moorish Science Temple after Ali. In later years, the group changed its name to the Nation of Islam.

Fard and Muhammad taught that Christianity was responsible for enslaving blacks and that blacks must stop looking to whites for employment and justice. The message of the Nation of Islam was especially attractive to inner-city black males. It taught that the black man was superior to the white man and that the black man was the original man. These teachings sounded good to some groups of African Americans. Their experiences of racism and hatred from the dominant culture helped influence them to accept a religion that taught black supremacy.

Malcolm X (born Malcolm Little and also known as Malik El-Shabazz) joined the Nation of Islam and became its most powerful representative. He gave new meaning to black pride during the civil rights years. In 1964, Malcolm and Muhammad had a parting of ways, however, after Malcolm went on a *pilgrimage* to Mecca. While he was there, Islam impressed him with its acceptance of all races, and he converted to mainstream Islam. When he returned to the United States, he dropped his black supremacist teachings. He wanted to bring Black Islam into union with traditional Muslims. A murderer cut his life and dream short soon after his return to the United States. Eventually, the

RELIGION & MODERN CULTURE

"We have as much right biblically and otherwise to believe that God is a Negro as white people have to believe that God is a fine-looking, symmetrical, and ornamental white man."

—Henry McNeal Turner, African American minister and activist

son of Elijah Muhammad, W. D. Muhammad, took over leadership of the group. Following in the footsteps of Malcolm X, he, too, wanted a religion that included people of all races.

THE IMPORTANCE OF THE BLACK CHURCH IN AFRICAN AMERICAN COMMUNITIES TODAY

"The Black church of the 20th century was . . . school, community center, meeting ground, political engine, restorer of hope," writes Kelly Starling in *Ebony* magazine. Black pastors today take care of much more than just sermons on Sunday. Reverend Lola, for example, pastor of a black community church in the southern United States, is a busy woman. She says God directed her to take care of the needs of the community around her church, and she has been obeying him ever since. She takes groceries to the needy, takes **prayer walks** around the area, and cares for the prostitutes and drug addicts in the neighborhood.

A study in 2000, conducted by the Interdenominational Theological Center (ITC), showed that 76 percent of black churches were involved in some type of voter registration service, and 75 percent had soup kitchens or food pantries. Ninety-two percent of black churches provide youth programs. Eighty-two percent give cash assistance to needy people. Reverend Stephen Rasor of ITC believes the reason why black

> *"God is a means of liberation and not a means to control others."*
>
> —*James Baldwin, African American author and activist*

churches are so socially minded is because their members have always struggled in this society in many ways. Leaders of black churches believe God is calling them to liberate and transform people and institutions. Michael Dash, associate professor at ITC, says, "Black Christianity has been a source, the primary consistent source, for African-American culture." He goes on to say it gives a framework that helps people combine their finances, blend ideas, and unify behind their leaders.

SANTERIA

It is not easy to find traces of the Santeria religion; there are not many churches or notices of religious services. However, if a person looks hard enough, she might notice small shops called *botanicas* in New York City. These structures provide a hint that the religion is alive. In them, one will find images of Catholic saints, musical instruments, candles, herbs, potions, and cauldrons—items used in Santeria worship.

Santeria began in West Africa with the Yoruba people. Spaniards brought West African slaves to Cuba, but slave owners did not allow slaves to practice their religions. The Africans adapted to their new circumstances. Although they acted as if they were worshipping Catholic saints, in reality they were worshipping *Orishas*, minor deities in their native religion. Each saint had an Orisha attached to it. The Spanish slave masters observed the Africans worshipping the saints, and named the practice Santeria, meaning "the way of the saints." Other names for the religion are *Regala de Ocha* (Rule of the Orisha) and *Lukumi*, a

49

RELIGION & MODERN CULTURE

"Remember that in a contest with oppression, the Almighty has no attribute which can take sides with oppressors."

—Frederick Douglass, *African American abolitionist and journalist*

Yoruba word that means friend. You can read more about Santeria in *The Growth of North American Religious Beliefs: Spiritual Diversity*, another book in this series.

Legal controversies have sprung up regarding religious freedom for Santerians. The Supreme Court ruled in favor of the Santeria church of Lukumi Babalu Aye in Hialeah, Florida, concerning animal sacrifice. The town had an ordinance against unnecessarily killing, tormenting, torturing, or mutilating an animal in a public or private ritual not for the primary purpose of eating the meat, but the Court ruled this ordinance could not apply to the Santerian church. The members say they sacrifice animals in a quick, humane way, with as little pain as possible for the creature.

Steve Quintana is priest of a Boston Santerian church and serves as unofficial spokesperson for Santerians in the United States. Quintana says Santeria is Mother Nature's religion. Some Americans are interested in ancient tribal alternative religions. Both Hispanics and blacks have roots in this religion, and some people of color have an interest in exploring their religious roots. Some find comfort in returning to religious and cultural ways of their pasts. They see them as links to who they are today.

African Americans have been a part of North America for centuries. In comparison, other national groups have been here only a short while. Arab Muslims, Coptic Christians, Zoroastrians, and members of other ancient Eastern faiths are also part of North American culture.

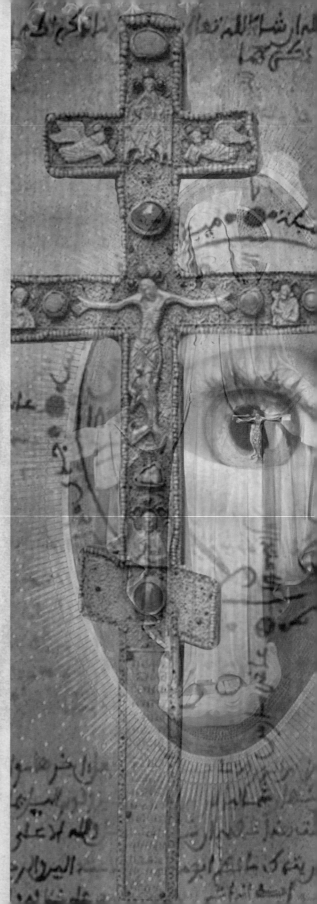

Chapter 4

RELIGION & MODERN CULTURE

LATINOS—BELIEVERS IN THE SAINTS & THE SPIRIT

The founders of an old Catholic church in the North Bronx of New York City named their church after an Irish saint, an appropriate gesture since the founders were Irish immigrants. Now, however, the English-language mass is attended by few people, mostly elderly. Worshippers prefer to listen to the hymns rather than sing, and they turn in their pews and exchange brief polite handshakes during greeting time.

After the mass ends and worshippers exit, the church quickly fills with a crowd for the Spanish-language mass. The church added this service only a few years ago, but it outgrew the English one almost overnight. These Spanish-speaking Catholics are of Mexican, Puerto Rican, and Dominican descent. They are young—moms and dads in their twenties, pushing strollers and carrying little children. The music contrasts with that of the English mass: worshippers sing with gusto along with a group of guitarists. At greeting time, people wander all over the room, hugging each other, kissing babies' cheeks, and expressing affection. Two things are apparent: a huge influx of members has rejuvenated this long-established Catholic congregation, and these members have brought a new boisterous sense of what it means to be Catholic.

This change is happening all over the United States. Today there are almost 26 million Catholic Latinos in the United States, an incredible influx for the Church.

The saying goes "nine months after Columbus, the first *mestizo* was born." Shortly after Columbus reached the New World, colonists from Spain and Portugal had children with the indigenous people of the New World. A century before the Pilgrims arrived in Plymouth, Massachusetts, Spanish colonists had already settled in the southern half of what is today the United States. European settlers also had children with Africans, whom they brought as slaves. From these unions, a new people emerged—*la Raza Mestizo* (the mixed race).

In the early twentieth century, civil war caused many Mexicans to flee across the borders of California, Arizona, and Texas to escape the violence in their homeland. In the 1980s, the Mexican economy went into a depression, and brutal wars engulfed Guatemala, El Salvador, and Nicaragua. Families fleeing poverty and warfare headed for *El Norte* (the North, the United States).

Latinos are the dominant minority group in the United States at the beginning of the twenty-first century. In January of 2003, the U.S. Census Bureau announced, "Hispanics have surpassed blacks as the nation's largest minority group. . . . Hispanics now comprise nearly 13

charismatic: Christian groups or worship characterized by a quest for inspired and ecstatic experiences such as healing, prophecy, and speaking in tongues.

mestizo: Someone whose parents or ancestors come from a mixture of European Spanish, Native, and African origins.

percent of the U.S. population." Later, the Census Bureau reported the Latino population in the United States nearly doubled between 1990 and 2004—from 22.4 million to almost 40 million.

The Hispanic population in Canada is much less significant proportionately. A 2003 report indicated there were 177,000 Hispanics in Canada, which is .06 of the Canadian population. Canada may be a cultural "salad bowl," but it does not have much salsa. To put things in another perspective, Latinos in the United States outnumber the entire population of Canada by 4 million people.

According to an August 2004 Barna Group survey, Hispanics are the least likely ethnic group to be aligned with a non-Christian faith. They are more likely than Anglo-Americans or Asian Americans to pray or read their Bible each week. They are also more likely to believe the Bible is literally true.

Latinos are not all Catholic, nor are they all Christian. The majority, however (almost 70 percent), remain loyal to the Catholic Church. An increasing number (at least 25 percent) are Pentecostal. Small numbers are of other faiths, most notably Santeria and Islam.

LATINOS—BELIEVERS IN THE SAINTS & THE SPIRIT

Father Lorenzo Miranda is pastor at St. Louis of France Catholic Church in La Puente, California. Thousands of families attend the church, most of them first-generation Central American immigrants. It is a challenge keeping up with the sheer number of people. Father Lorenzo says, "I could work all day and stay here 'til midnight, just receiving people." At the same time, Father Lorenzo loves his work. He says, "Ministry is not like making cars or something—you can't measure the way it changes people!" However, he does see the difference faith makes in people's lives.

TRADICIÓNES (TRADITIONS)

Latino Catholics share many beliefs in common with Catholics from other cultural backgrounds. However, Latino Catholics bring their own special traditions and practices. Folk masses, with guitar music and hand clapping, are common. Father Lorenzo says, "They make the mass like a fiesta."

Latinos also bring their own sacred customs to North America. Among these are processions. Professor Richard Wightman Fox, who teaches religion at the University of Southern California and is author of the popular book *Jesus in America*, describes one procession in the Colonia neighborhood of Oxnard, California:

A bearded, barefoot Jesus in a long white robe and a crown of thorns drags his cross slowly down Juanita Avenue. Roman soldiers right on his heels are whipping his red-stained back. His eyes are cast down. Hundreds of the faithful, including a throng of children, press tightly behind the soldiers. Residents stand on balconies, and shoppers clog sidewalks in front of Lupita's Panderia and Garcia's Discoteca y Video.

"We are Mestizo Christians, and this Mestizo tra-dition can enrich the Protestant and Catholic Traditions of the United States."
—*Virgilio Elizondo, professor, University of Notre Dame*

Such processions make it possible for Hispanic Catholics to experience Bible events as though they were happening today. Many people in the broader population had experiences of this sort when they saw the movie *The Passion of the Christ.*

Latino Catholics have a special love for the saints, and especially for the Virgin of Guadalupe. Father Lorenzo says:

The Santos [saints] are concrete human beings, like all of us. When we see them with their struggles and virtues, we recall how we also struggle with the good and bad within ourselves. The saints come from every background of life, so all kinds of people can relate to them.

Hispanics' most beloved saint is the Queen of Heaven, especially in her identity as the Virgin of Guadalupe. In Latino neighborhoods around the country, her picture appears on buildings, businesses, walls, hats, cars, tattooed arms—all over. She is so renowned in Mexico that Mexicans sometimes call themselves *Guadalupeños.*

According to tradition, the Virgin appeared to Juan Diego, an Aztec peasant, in 1531. The Virgin took the form of a dark-skinned Indian girl. She spoke to Juan Diego in his native Nahuatl language and gave him a miraculous sign. She told him to fill his cactus-fiber cape (*tilma*) with flowers. He went to the bishop in Mexico City, shook out his cape, and

"The first priority of the church must always be the needs of the poor, the immigrant, the abandoned, the unwanted and those in special need. This is the first priority of the Gospel and it must be ours today. We must not only minister to the needs of the poor but recognize how the poor minister to the rest of the church."

—Virgilio Elizondo, professor, University of Notre Dame

the perfect image of the Virgin appeared on it. To this day, millions of worshippers come to Mexico City to honor the image of the Virgin on the tilma.

The dark-skinned Virgin (*La Morenita*) has held a special place in Latino hearts for more than four centuries. Affectionate followers also call her *Neustra Señora*, "Our Lady."

Virgilio Elizondo, professor at the University of Notre Dame, explains that Mexican Americans are proud of their mestizo heritage, a rich combination of European and Native American blood. He says the Virgin of Guadalupe is a mestiza, "the first truly American person and as such the mother of the new generations to come." According to Father Lorenzo:

Our Lady has always been there in the struggle for justice. In the independence struggle in Mexico, the people carried a banner of our lady. You see images of her in all the different places where people work. There is a very deep connection between the experience of work and her presence.

AN UNOFFICIAL BUT HELPFUL SAINT— TORIBIO ROMO

Many of the santos are "official" saints recognized by the Catholic Church. Others are "folk traditions"—beliefs that come from experiences of the common people. According to an often-told tale, a young man was in trouble crossing from Mexico to the United States sometime around 1980. When he was lost in the desert, a young man came and helped him find his path. After seeing him safely to his destination, this helpful stranger told the new immigrant to return someday to Santa Ana de Guadalupe and pay him respects. "Ask for Señor Romo—that is my name." Years later, the young man did so. He asked all over, but could not find Señor Romo. Finally, a woman showed him a picture. "Yes, that is the man!" The woman was shocked. "That is impossible," she said. "This is Toribio Romo, the young priest who was martyred in 1928. He is buried at the church here." Ever since, Latino immigrants crossing the border have sought the help of Saint Toribio Romo.

"A good deed is the best prayer."

—*Mexican proverb*

Leaders of the U.S. Catholic Church are thankful for the influx of new worshippers, but there have also been some tensions. Virgilio Elizondo writes in the book *El Cuerpo De Cristo*:

I often have the feeling that the U.S. Catholic Church wants us, but not as Hispanics with our tradition of faith, our language, our customs, music, sense of beauty, and our festivals. Our God-designed culture with its rich religious culture is still looked upon as backward and alien . . . by many in the Church.

Despite some concerns, Latino Catholics have made a huge impact on the Church—one largely recognized as positive.

HOLY SPIRIT CHURCHES

A century ago, practically all Hispanics throughout the Americas were Catholic. During the past decade, Pentecostal churches have exploded in Central and South America. Mision Carismatica Internacional Church in Colombia has over 400,000 members. A 2004 survey found more Pentecostals than practicing Catholics in Guatemala. This Pentecostal explosion in Latin America has influenced Latino faith in *Los Estados Unidos* (the United States) as well. More than nine million U.S. Hispanics are Pentecostal (or **charismatic**, which means nearly the same thing) Christians. Most Latinos who attend Pentecostal churches refer to themselves simply as "Cristiano" (Christian). Pentecostal churches draw many converts with their emphasis that God is able to work powerfully in believers' lives, through his Holy Spirit.

The word "Pentecostal" comes from chapter 2 of the book of Acts in the New Testament where the Holy Spirit came upon the followers of Christ after he ascended into heaven. The Holy Spirit gave believers the ability to speak in unfamiliar languages and to perform miracles. These same actions are part of Pentecostal spirituality today. Pentecostal and charismatic churches share with Catholics belief in the Trinity (God is Father, Son, and Holy Spirit) and in the need to share the love of Christ through loving deeds of service. In other respects, however, they differ from Catholicism. Pentecostals do not ask the saints or the Virgin Mary to pray for them; they believe one should pray directly to God the Father through Christ. The concept of conversion is also different. Catholics teach that one grows into relationship with God through a process involving the sacraments (sacred rituals) of the church. These include confession, baptism, and the mass. Pentecostals say a person becomes Christian simply by inviting Jesus into his or her heart. If a person prays in this way, they become "born again" —that is, they begin a new kind of spiritual life.

Templo Calvario, a Pentecostal church in Santa Ana, California, is the fastest growing Latino church in the United States. In 2004, over 10,000 people attended the church weekly. Under the leadership of Pastor Daniel De Leon, the church has grown from just 135 people three decades ago. It prides itself on being "bicultural and bilingual," yet the majority of attendees are Hispanic. Templo Calvario has organized a network of churches in southern California that provide food to 80,000 people every month.

Victory Outreach is another outstanding Latino Pentecostal church. In 1967, a young heroin addict named Sonny Arguinzoni had a conversion experience and found freedom from drugs. Sonny bought a house in the Boyle Heights section of Los Angeles, where many young Latinos struggled with poverty, drugs, and gangs. He brought struggling teens to live there and straighten out their lives. From this humble beginning, Victory Outreach has grown into a major Pentecostal movement. In

"Let not your heart be disturbed. Do not fear sickness, nor any other anguish. Am I not here, who is your Mother? Are you not under my protection? Am I not your health? Are you not happily within my fold? What else do you wish? Do not grieve nor be disturbed by anything."

—*words said by Our Lady of Guadalupe to Juan Diego*

2004, it had over 200,000 members in more than 500 churches. The Victory Outreach Web site says:

> We have grown into one of the largest inner-city ministries and Pentecostal denominations in the world, meeting the needs of people from all walks of life. For 37 years, Victory Outreach has trained and equipped men and women to reach their full potential in life, whether it is establishing a church, building a business, or growing and nurturing a family.

Templo Calvario and Victory Outreach highlight the tremendous growth of Latino Pentecostal churches in recent years. However, they are not typical of the movement. Most Pentecostal Latino churches have a hundred or less members. These smaller churches grow and reproduce quickly. In other words, the fast growth of Latino Pentecostalism has occurred by means of small churches spreading rapidly. In major U.S. cities, two or three Pentecostal churches often meet in storefronts on the same street.

THE SUFFERING GOD

Hispanic churches may differ from one another theologically, but they share a common commitment to social justice. Homeboy Industries, for example, in the Boyle Heights section of Los Angeles, provides gang members a chance to start a new life. Every month, more than a thousand Latino gang members walk through its doors hoping to begin anew. Homeboy Industries helps them find work, counseling, or tattoo removal. Most important, Jesuit Father Greg Boyle founded Homeboy Industries on the idea of a God who loves everyone "no matter what." His ministry is a place where the violence of East Los Angeles transforms into a vision of God's peaceful Kingdom.

An hour drive south, in Santa Ana, several hundred people gather every Tuesday morning at Obras de Amor (Works of Love) warehouse, a ministry of Templo Calvario. Some of these men and women are homeless, others lack transportation or decent paying jobs. They are all races, though predominantly Latino. Every week, Obras de Amor gives away more than twenty tons of food at this site. They only employ one worker, but every week more than seventy volunteers help distribute food. A frequently heard expression at Obras de Amor is "*Soy bendicido, para bendecir*" (I am blessed to bless others).

Latinos are not only changing the way churches in America do things, they are also influencing the way churches think about God. Latino theology was formed by the experiences of common people, rather than the insights of learned scholars. Virgilio Elizondo says, "My father hardly knew how to read, but his understanding of God is still my own most precious understanding of God today—far richer than any I have ever encountered in the best theologians I have ever read or studied."

The experiences of the common people in the Latino religious tradition convince them God cares for those who suffer. People who have suffered injustice realize God suffers injustice with them. Justo Gonzalez writes in his book *Mañana: Christian Theology from a Hispanic Perspective*, "The God of the Bible is also . . . the victim of history. Inasmuch as God suffers oppression and injustice . . . the suffering Christ is important to Hispanics because he is the sign that God suffers with us."

Chapter 5

ANGLO-AMERICAN FAITH
Heritage & Change

RELIGION & MODERN CULTURE

The big white bus was messy and smelly. It looked as if more than thirty teenagers had been living in the bus, driving through the desert, going days without showers. In fact, that was the case. The youth group from a large evangelical church in northern Arizona decided to spend their winter break from school doing something for others. They raised money for the trip selling candy and washing cars. With a small team of adult youth leaders, they drove two days south into a barren part of Mexico. There, they worked in the hot sun building cement walls for a new orphanage. After sweaty workdays, they took "spit baths" with water from a faucet and drove to the nearest town.

There, they sang Christian songs in the plaza and tried to use their high school Spanish to talk with people from the village. This group of teens from a largely Caucasian American church was carrying on a tradition of *evangelism* and ministry that began centuries before them.

CAUCASIAN RELIGION BY THE NUMBERS

Protestants are non-Catholic Christians, a group that is often lumped into two categories: evangelical and mainline churches. The term evangelical refers to Christians who regard the Bible as literal truth, emphasize the need for a personal relationship with God, and try to share this good news by word and deed. Mainline believers are those who regard the Bible as important but not literally true, believe God has a relationship with people in a variety of religions, and emphasize the importance of social issues. Many Christians hold combinations of these views, and some avoid evangelical or mainline labels.

White, non-Hispanics account for 69 percent of the U.S. population and 86 percent of the Canadian population. According to a 2001 survey by the Pew Research Center, 82 percent of U.S. citizens of all races define themselves as Christians. Of those, 23 percent define themselves as white evangelical Protestants; 19 percent as white mainline Protestants; 9 percent as black Protestants; 23 percent as Roman Catholics; and 6 percent as other Christians, including Eastern Orthodox and Mormons.

In Canada, 77 percent of the population (all races) consider themselves Christian. There is a higher percentage of Roman Catholics in Canada than in the United States—41 percent of Canadian Christians. Evangelicals are fewer in Canada than in the United States. Many of the earliest French settlers in Canada were Catholic, and Quebec still has a strong sense of Catholic religious identity.

The United States also has a sizable Jewish population—approximately 5.2 million. Most are of European background. Jewish believers have lived in North America since colonial times. Many have come recently from the former Soviet republics. The Canadian Jewish population is 360,000. Jewish synagogues, like Christian churches, vary from *conservative* to *liberal* in both politics and beliefs.

ANGLO CHRISTIAN HERITAGE

The history of white Christians in North America is full of *paradoxes*. On the one hand, European colonists enslaved minorities. At the same

73

> *"The test of a preacher is that his congregation goes away not saying 'What a lovely sermon!' but 'I will do something.'"*
>
> —*Billy Graham, American evangelist*

time, other white people of faith led the fight to end slavery. Anglo Christians have sometimes been intolerant of other religions; the Salem witch trials are the worst example. Yet they founded a nation that champions liberty.

Religious revivals played a major role in U.S. history. On the frontier in the eighteenth and nineteenth centuries, Protestant preachers would come to towns and speak at large outdoor gatherings called "camp meetings." Revival preachers emphasized that each individual man, woman, and child had to decide whether to live for God. Revivals often had a lasting effect on morals in a community. In some cases, crime and drunkenness disappeared from entire communities. Some historians believe the moral and industrial strength of early America was a result of these religious revivals.

White evangelicals in the nineteenth century were highly involved in issues of social justice. Quakers and evangelical revival preachers led the fight to abolish slavery. White Protestants in the early 1800s also began many hospitals, orphanages, schools, and soup kitchens. Many early evangelicals believed making the world a better place was a necessary part of Christian faith. Today, increasing numbers of evangelicals (along with mainline Protestants and Catholic Christians) are involved in combating poverty and AIDS as well as with other vital social issues. One of the best known of these is Jim Wallis, the author of the best-selling book *God's Politics*. Wallis argues that God is not a Democrat or a Republican. He believes Christians should support life consistently. To do this, they should be both antiwar (like many Democrats) and antiabortion (like many Republicans).

READING, WRITING, & RELIGION

The Puritans and Pilgrims based religious authority entirely on the Bible—not on church traditions, as in the Catholic and Anglican churches. Puritans believed it was necessary for every citizen to be able to read, since if a person could not read, he could not hear God speak to him through the Bible. For this reason, the English colonies placed unusual emphasis on education. Three prestigious universities in the United States—Harvard, Princeton, and Yale—were founded as religious institutions. The value placed on literacy and the high degree of literacy in Anglo-American society began with this religious demand for education.

TRENDS IN ANGLO-AMERICAN RELIGION TODAY

In the United States, the evangelical tradition is especially influential. Political analysts say President George W. Bush's reelection in 2004 was probably due to white evangelical voters. The majority of evangelicals are politically conservative and agree with the president's opposition to same-sex marriage and abortion.

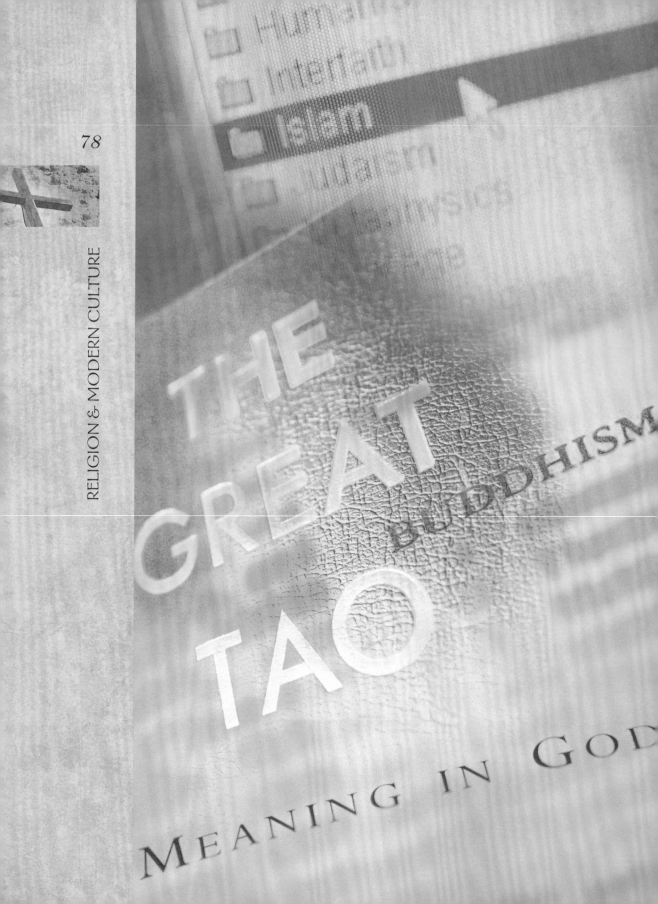

RELIGION & MODERN CULTURE

THE GREAT TAO

BUDDHISM

MEANING IN GOD

"No man ever loved like Jesus. He taught the blind to see and the dumb to speak. He died on the cross to save us. He bore our sins. And now God says, 'Because He did, I can forgive you.'"

—Billy Graham, American evangelist

At the same time, the beliefs of Anglo-Americans are becoming more diverse. Within evangelicalism, many disagree with conservative political views or doubt common doctrines. The average age of evangelicals is growing older; many young people are choosing beliefs that differ from those of their parents.

Anglo-Americans are increasingly attracted to non-Western religions. Though numbers are still small, more Anglo-Americans are putting their faith in Buddhism, Islam, Wicca, and other nontraditional religions.

While faith in organized religion is declining, spiritual interest is increasing. Popular music contains many spiritual themes. The Irish rock band U2, for example, continues to be hugely popular in the United States, and many of their songs have Christian themes. Lead singer Bono met with Pope John Paul II (and exchanged a pair of his signature sunglasses for rosary beads). Catholic producer and actor Mel Gibson had a huge hit with his independently produced film *The Passion of the Christ.* Jesus is even popular on T-shirts, and religion is one of the most explored topics by teens on the Internet.

Fortunately, it is becoming more difficult to speak of "white" churches or "white Christian" beliefs. Religious leaders are working to grow churches that reflect the multiracial societies of Canada and the United States.

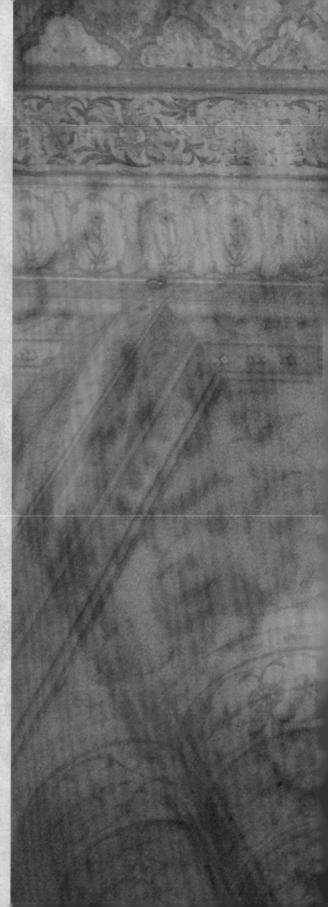

MIDDLE EASTERN MIX

"I would have preferred to stay in my house . . . but I put a gold ribbon on a coffee cake I had baked, walked up her front steps and knocked on her door. I introduced myself and handed her the cake . . . she seemed pleased and surprised." Kaye shared her experience of meeting her new Middle Eastern, Muslim neighbor in a *Christianity Today* magazine article. Hafsa, the new neighbor, showed Kaye a picture of Jesus and Mary hanging on the wall. "I believe in all the Prophets of God, they are all from God," she shared. Before Kaye went home, Hafsa gave her a book to read about Islam. Kaye promised to read it and bring it back. As Kaye was leaving, Hafsa invited Kaye and her husband to come have dinner with them sometime soon. It was a small step to take, but it was the beginning of getting to know and understand her new immigrant neighbor.

RELIGION & MODERN CULTURE

"Man is created in the image of God. Accordingly, all persons irrespective of background are my brothers and sisters, because they are in the image of God, the Creator."

—Bernard Sabella, a Christian living in Jerusalem and working with Palestinian refugees, quoted in Christianity Today, *December 2002*

DEMOGRAPHICS OF MIDDLE EASTERN IMMIGRATION

According to the Center for Immigration Studies (CIS), Middle Easterners are one of the fastest-growing immigrant groups in the United States. There were approximately 1.5 million Middle Eastern immigrants in 2000, up from less than 200,000 in 1970. If the trend continues, by 2010, there will be 1.1 million more in the United States. According to the CIS, out of these immigrants, approximately 73 percent are Muslim.

The DanielPipes.Org Web site says that in 2002 approximately two million Muslims lived in the United States, about 1 percent of the population. Other estimates suggest two or three times that number; counting religious adherents is always difficult. The three largest groups come from South Asia, Iran, and the Arab-speaking countries. The largest group is from South Asia (Bangladesh, India, and Pakistan). As is common with immigrant groups, Muslims are younger than the national average of the populace in the United States. There are more Muslim males than females; usually immigrant men come first and women follow. The largest concentrations of Arabs live in the Detroit area. The state with the largest Middle Eastern population is California, but Virginia has the fastest-growing community of Middle Easterners.

The country from which most Muslims come is Pakistan, followed by Bangladesh, Iran, Iraq, Turkey, and Egypt.

Canada is also a country with a large immigrant population. In 2001, Canada admitted approximately 250,000 immigrants. Of those immigrants, 53 percent were from Asia and the Pacific, and 19 percent were from the Middle East and Africa. Canada hopes to increase their skilled labor force from these immigrants. However, foreign doctors and engineers often have a difficult time passing Canadian regulations in their fields.

RELIGIOUS TRENDS AMONG MUSLIM IMMIGRANTS

When Muslim immigrants come to North America, they tend to either leave their religion or become more religious. Some, once they have the freedom to decide their own way, leave Islam, choosing instead to "fit in" with the differing values and beliefs of Western culture. However, there are cultural and moral reasons why other Muslims become more religious. From a cultural standpoint, because North American ways are so different, many want to cling to familiar rituals and customs and spend more time at mosques. From a moral standpoint, when immigrants see the openness of the North American secular culture, they also may grow stronger in the values of their Muslim faith. One Muslim told the *New York Times*, "When I came to America I really became a Muslim. Back home, I took it for granted."

According to surveys, in the United States about as many Muslims live by the laws of Islam as those who do not. One-third of Muslim women obey the Islamic order not to wear makeup in public. A third of Muslim women also follow the Muslim rule of not shaking hands with a male who is not part of their family. About 25 percent of Muslim schoolgirls wear a head covering. Prayers usually drop among immi-

grants; approximately 10 percent of Muslims go to Friday prayers at mosques. Drinking alcohol is common among some Muslims in North America, and many young Muslim men violate premarital sexual standards. It is difficult to avoid the temptations of Western culture.

Many Muslim parents are concerned; they want their children to keep their faith. These parents strive to bring up children who are respectful, hardworking, honest, and modest. They see many American children as disrespectful, unwilling to work, and arrogant. Some Muslim parents put their children in Islamic schools to try to protect them from U.S. and Canadian culture. Sometimes Muslim kids try to hide their faith from non-Muslim friends in order to be "cool." They may only wear their head covering at home, or change into tighter clothes once they reach the public school. They may claim they are dieting during Ramadan (a time when Muslims fast). Other young people, however, are proud of their faith.

Cultural practices and religion are closely tied for Middle Eastern Muslims. After migrating to the United States, it is difficult for parents and children to adjust to living in a culture so different from their own. One young Arab woman tells how her family expects their children to go to school, come home to help with the family business, then go to the mosque, and finally home to study. That was her whole life growing up. She spent her time almost solely with family and relatives. Her family believed this was one way to keep their children pure and free from the negative values of the dominant culture. Those who deepen in their Islamic faith find comfort in the familiarity of religion and customs they grew up with. They have a bond with other Muslims that shields them from the harshness of a new culture.

Islamic believers from various areas hold differing customs. For this reason, Muslim immigrants to North America may experience tensions with fellow believers coming from other countries. For example, Turkish Muslims put up gravestones with photographs laminated on them when a loved one dies—but this is offensive to Arab Muslims.

THE QUR'AN—PRICELESS

If a person is looking to buy a Qur'an in a bookstore, they will not find a price tag on the scriptures. Instead, it is appropriate to ask the clerk what the proper "gift" for the book would be. Muslims believe that no price can be put to their sacred scriptures.

Arabs speak the language of the Qur'an, and they are proud of this. Non-Arab Muslims sometimes feel that Arabic-speakers look down on them. Some Muslim parents who may not mind if their son marries a non-Muslim American girl would mind him marrying a Muslim girl from a different sect.

OTHER ANCIENT EASTERN FAITHS

Zoroastrianism is a religion that originated in Persia—what is now Iran—in the sixth century BCE. Zoroastrians regard their founder, Zoroaster, as a prophet. Their sacred scriptures are called the Avestam, and they believe in living an industrious, honest, and most of all, charitable life. Their religion encourages them to have good thoughts, good words, and to do good deeds.

Approximately 200,000 Zoroastrians exist in the world today: 60,000 in India, 90,000 in Iran, and 15,000 in Canada and the United

States. The Zoroastrians who came to North America began migrating in the 1950s and 1960s to obtain higher education and take advantage of better business opportunities. With them came their faith, literature, customs, culture, and language. The most well-known Zoroastrians are Zubin Mehta, the former conductor of both the Los Angeles symphony and New York Philharmonic orchestras, and the late Freddie Mercury of the rock band Queen.

MIDDLE EASTERN CHRISTIANITY

The day after September 11, 2001, students at a Catholic college asked a Middle Eastern classmate, "Father, are you Muslim?" He chuckled and pointed to the cross he was wearing, "Muslims don't believe in the cross. If I am a Muslim, I don't wear a cross." In fact, he was a priest from one of the ancient Christian churches. Seventy percent of all Middle Eastern immigrants are Christians, according to *Christianity Today*'s April 2004 issue. They are scattered across the United States in over four hundred churches of various denominations. Among these are seven groups: Antiochian Orthodox, Coptic, Melkite, Chaldean, Maronite, Syriac, and Assyrian Orthodox traditions.

All these churches can trace their origins to earliest Christianity. The Coptic Church says the Apostle Mark began their church in Egypt. The Syriac Orthodox Church claims to have records of correspondence between Jesus and one of their kings. Scholars debate whether such traditions are historically true, but both churches' origins are surely ancient.

Christians in the Arab world have come through a tumultuous history: First, the Roman Empire persecuted them. Then, the Syriac, Coptic, and Assyrian groups split from the Roman and Eastern Orthodox Churches. In the eighth and ninth centuries, Islam took over two-thirds of what had been the Christian world. All of this took its toll

U.S. & CANADIAN COPTIC CHRISTIANS

The Coptic Church teaches charitable giving, and U.S. and Canadian Coptic members participate in organizations called BLESS Canada, and BLESS U.S.A. These nonprofit charity organizations raise money for needy Coptic Church members in Egypt. BLESS stands for Bishopric of Public, Ecumenical and Social Services. BLESS Canada sends all of its funds to the Agape Program of the Charity Department. This department assists very poor villages in Egypt become established, self-sufficient, and productive communities. The following Bible verse is on the BLESS Canada Web site: "Stretch out your hand to the poor, so that your blessing may be complete" (Sirach 7:32).

on Middle Eastern Christian churches, and they became separated from mainstream Christianity. Their original worship language disappeared as Arab languages took over. The Muslim world did not allow them to evangelize, so their numbers dropped.

The twentieth century has also been harsh on Middle Eastern Christians. Wars between Arab countries, wars with Israel, and persecutions have forced millions of Eastern Christians to leave their countries. Ten to twelve million Copts are still in Egypt, where they have a

91

certain amount of political influence and are legally protected. In other Arab nations, however, more Christians have left than have stayed. Six million Christians have moved out of Lebanon; less than two million Christians have stayed there.

Though Middle Eastern Christians have more economic and religious freedom in North America than in their home countries, the picture is not all rosy. Elesha Coffman writes in her article "Lost in America," in *Christianity Today*, April 2004: "Like all immigrants, Arab Christians struggle to get all of their paperwork in order, to find jobs and housing, to communicate in a second language, and to establish social connections." She goes on to report how Arab Christians have suffered. Since September 11, 2001, Middle Eastern Christians are seen as Muslim by the North American populace, which means they may face prejudice along with their Muslim brothers and sisters. Non-Arabs scrutinize them more closely because they are Arab, yet they are ignored by some fellow immigrants because they are not Muslim.

Susan, a Coptic college student at Duke University, shared her experience of living in North America in *Christianity Today* magazine's March 26, 2004, issue. Her family moved from Egypt to the United States when she was thirteen years old, but they still practice their faith. For instance, Copts attend a four-hour service every Sunday. On Saturday night, the vespers service lasts only one hour, but then worshippers are expected to stay for the midnight praises that last several hours. The midnight service attendance is usually low. Susan told of how beautiful the service is but how difficult it is to sit for the long hours.

The church preaches against the five Ds—dancing, drinking, drugs, dressing provocatively, and dating. Coptic teens have a hard time living in the West and abiding by the church's standards. Susan admires those who can put up with the pressure in this society and still live the Coptic Church principles, but she is not sure she can do this. Susan believes the Western Coptic Church has made concessions to keep members. For example, in Egypt, couples who divorce for reasons the church does not approve of cannot take communion; in North America, they can.

In Canada and the United States, we have the privilege of knowing many immigrants from various backgrounds. Learning more about their beliefs, we can gain deeper understanding of our own. It is especially illuminating watching how immigrants' spiritual beliefs change as they encounter North American culture. Consider your own spiritual beliefs. Do the teachings of your religion conflict with popular culture in your country?

Chapter 7

THE ASIAN CONTRIBUTION

RELIGION & MODERN CULTURE

Someone sitting in the Long Beach Asian Pacific Mental Health Department might blink twice at seeing a psychologist walk by with a shaved head, clad in sandals and a long saffron-colored robe. They would be seeing Dr. Kong Chhean, a Buddhist monk/psychologist. Dr. Chhean leads a complicated life joining two worlds together. His day begins with rituals he performs at the large Buddhist temple of Khemara Buddhikarama. He then leaves for his other job as a mental-health services coordinator at the Long Beach Asian Pacific Mental Health Department. At lunch, he returns to the temple for his last meal of the day; he has taken a monk's vow to never eat after lunch.

Dr. Chhean says his most important work is helping Cambodian people adjust to their new lives in the United States. Most of the immigrants in his community arrived there as illiterate farmers. They were from rural areas, so they needed help adjusting to their new urban surroundings. As is common in most cultures, parents and teenagers have trouble relating to each other. However, the usual problems of dating and homework issues are intensified because of cultural issues. Dr. Chhean has started counseling programs, parenting programs, alcohol programs, and support programs for the elderly. Preserving Buddhist faith in the United States is very important for Cambodian immigrants. Some believe that if Cambodians leave their Buddhist faith, they lose their traditional culture, because Buddhism is its foundation.

STATISTICS ON ASIAN & SOUTHEAST ASIAN IMMIGRATION

The 2000 Census records state ten to twelve million people of Asian origin live in the United States. Within this group are Chinese (2.3 million), Filipinos (1.9 million), Asian Indians (1.7 million), Vietnamese (1.1 million), Koreans (1.1 million), and a smaller number of Japanese. Other groups that fit into this category are South Asians such as Indians, Pakistanis, Bangladeshis, and Sri Lankans. Also included are Thai, Burmese, Laotians, Cambodians, Hmong, Tibetans, and Nepalese immigrants. Pacific Islanders—Samoans, Tongans, Fijians, and Guamanians—are also counted as Asian immigrants.

Most Asian Americans live in urban areas, at least three-quarters of them in cities with more that two million people. Forty percent of Asian immigrants live around the areas of Los Angeles, San Francisco, and New York City. Half the Asian American population lives on the West Coast or Hawaii (5.2 million). More than four million live in California.

Almost three million Asian immigrants live in Canada's large cities.

GLOSSARY

Apostle Thomas: One of the original twelve followers of Christ.

caste system: Hindu hereditary social classes.

communist: A totalitarian system of government where private property does not exist.

individualistic: Stressing the importance of the individual rather than the community or the family.

Approximately half of this population is from China. Most of the 1.4 million Chinese immigrants are in Toronto or Vancouver. The current number of Japanese immigrants in Canada is 120,000, while Koreans number 130,000. The Vietnamese may be the fastest-growing Asian group; in 1996, their numbers were up to 170,000. Canada also has immigrants from Laos, Burma, Cambodia, Philippines, Malaysia, Thailand, and Indonesia.

Wherever Asian immigrants settle, they bring their rich cultures and religions with them. Almost every major world religion is represented in North America's Asian population. Asians comprise the largest Muslim group in the world, and Indonesia is the world's largest Muslim country. Other religions represented among Asians include Hindu, Buddhism, Daoism, Shinto, Janism, Sikh, Confucianism, and Christianity.

"[O God] since I have fallen at your feet, I do not care for anybody else."

—Rahras, a Sikh evening prayer

THE CHINESE & BUDDHISM

The first Chinese immigrants came to live in the United States in the 1800s. As their population grew, so did anti-Chinese sentiments. At that time, the United States passed laws to keep Chinese immigrants out of the country. Those who were already in the United States were restricted to living in certain areas. This is when Chinatowns developed in the United States. Historically, Chinese immigrants had only themselves and their faith for support. When the U.S. government made laws against them and they suffered from prejudice, Chinese immigrants had each other.

Chinatowns today are found in San Francisco, Boston, and New York. There are also Chinese-dominated suburbs such as Monterey Park in the Los Angeles area, where more than half the city is Chinese. Any Chinese immigrant who wishes to can live immersed in his or her own culture in these areas. Persons of Chinese background can find employment, social groups, education, and Buddhist religion in Chinatowns. Here, religion, culture, and family are interrelated. The stores and businesses in Chinatowns are usually family owned and operated, and in almost every business, there is a Buddhist shrine.

VIETNAMESE IMMIGRANTS

Asian immigrants also came to the United States from Vietnam, many because of the Vietnam War. By the end of 1975, 130,000 immigrants had arrived from Southeast Asia, and by the end of 1985, 643,000 were estimated to be in the United States. Five years later, the number had grown to over a million. These Vietnamese immigrants were either Roman Catholics or Buddhists.

Portland, Oregon, with about 40,000 Vietnamese, is the eighth-largest Vietnamese community in the United States. Over the years, the Portland immigrants have kept their Vietnamese identity and made a place for themselves in the dominant culture. The Portland Vietnamese immigrants came with their religious leaders. They have a Catholic priest, and elders and priests of the Buddhist community. In this and many other parts of the country, Buddhist communities are flourishing.

HINDUS IN NORTH AMERICA

Hinduism, the world's third-largest religion, is the main religion of India, Nepal, and the Tamils in Sri Lanka. It has about 762 million followers worldwide. Statistics differ, but the American Identification Religious Survey reported 766,000 Hindus in the United States and 157,015 in Canada in 2001.

In Diana Eck's book *A New Religious America*, she tells of a Hindu community in Boston. In the 1970s, many Hindus came to Boston as students, originally intending to return to India but then settling in the United States. A group of Tamil families from south India began meeting in each other's homes on special religious holidays. They realized their children needed ways to preserve their Hindu cultural and religious identities and decided to build a temple in their area—the New England Hindu Temple. They placed the Goddess Lakshmi in the sanctuary. The group picked her because she is the Goddess of Fortune and they believe she has blessed them in America. Each couple donated $101 to start their temple fund. By 1981, they had collected $30,000 in donations, enough to buy a plot of land.

The group brought a traditional Indian architect from India, and *shilpis* who were artisans. After months of intense building and decorating, the community of Hindus consecrated the temple. About three thousand Hindus from New England attended the ceremony, along with city council members and the mayor of Boston. In building the first temple in New England, they had also built a community.

Most of the families involved in the building project were not especially religious before coming to the United States. They probably would not have participated in such a project in their home country. Living in another culture caused them to appreciate their Hindu roots. In the 1980s and 1990s, many more Hindu temples have been constructed across the United States.

RELIGION & MODERN CULTURE

The name *Sikh* means learner. It is often mispronounced "seek," but the correct pronunciation is, "se-ikh." The founder was Shri Guru Nanak Dev Ji (1469–1538). One of the pillars of Sikhs is his saying, "There is no Hindu, there is no Muslim." He rejected idol worship and the *caste system* in India. He believed in one God—a formless being with many names. Today, there are 22.1 million Sikhs in the world, most of them living in Punjab, India. Sikh men are easily recognized because they do not cut their hair and they wear a turban.

Dr. Jasbir Singh Kang has lived in Yuba City, California, for the last fifteen years. He writes on Sikhe.com of the dilemma facing Sikhs in the United States and Canada: Sikhs need to look for long-term survival in North America and the world. They must work to enable both Sikhism and American culture to coexist. Dr. Kang thinks the group needs to make Sikhism compatible with American ways or future generations will be Americanized. Looking at the history of migration, one can see that in some cases this has happened already.

In 1890, the first Sikhs from Punjabi came to the United States. Because the United States did not allow them to return to their country to find wives, many of them married Mexican women or remained single. Children born of Mexican mothers were raised Catholic, and the Sikh religion was not carried on in their families. In a second wave of immigrants after 1948, children were raised with Punjabi mothers. There was a lack of *Gurdwaras* (places of worship), however, and much prejudice against them. Eventually, Sikhism among this group also died out. After 1965, many more Sikhs arrived. They were able to form pockets of Punjabi communities where pride in their traditional culture flourished.

Another wave of immigrants came after 1980, political victims from Punjab. These immigrants control most of the Gurdwaras in Canada and the United States today. The most recent immigrants seem to be

HINDUS IN CANADA

Hindus in Canada have a reputation for being more open minded and more liberal than those in other countries. One recent trend is for Canadian Hindu children to marry outside their religion. A volunteer Hindu priest said that three out of four marriages he performed in a year were mixed marriages. Usually this involves a Hindu marrying a white Christian; Hindu-Muslim marriages are not common.

Hindu parents are concerned about their children carrying on the Hindu religion. They want their culture to survive in Canada, and it will most likely do so. Canadians already know and enjoy Hindu concepts such as karma, reincarnation, and yoga. Hindus have a reputation for being an accepting religion; they believe there are many paths to God. Canadians look favorably on this liberal view.

the least interested in maintaining their Sikh ways. For example, many of the men cut their hair before they arrive.

As of the year 2000, approximately 100,000 Sikhs lived in the United States and 225,000 in Canada. Sikhs in the United States live mostly in California, New York, Texas, Michigan, and Illinois. In Yuba City, California, there are 10,000 Sikhs in a ten-mile radius, but less than one hundred attend weekly services at the Gurdwara. Thousands participate

in the cultural festivals, however. In 2001, Yuba City had a festival attended by 12,000 Sikhs and other interested Americans.

Jasbir Singh struggles with how best to Americanize the Sikh religion. He does not want to lose the essence of the faith. If the Yuba group changes too much, their own community will see them as outsiders. He ends by saying, "I am sure Sikhism is universal and we cannot tie it to Punjabi culture."

"I do not follow the religious ways preached by various religions believing in Ram, Mohammed, Puran or Qur'an. . . . I do not recognize any of these. O God, I have written these hymns with your grace and kindness. All that has been said is in fact spoken by you."

—Rahras, a Sikh evening prayer

ASIAN CHRISTIANS

The United States and Canada have churches from a broad variety of Asian ethnic groups. The Chinese Christian church, however, has one of the longest histories in North America. Dr. Samuel Ling, a historian, theologian, and ordained minister of the Presbyterian Church in America, says there are over one thousand Chinese Christian churches in the United States and Canada today. In an interview on the Christian Post Web site, Dr. Ling explained how important the church was in the days when the first Chinese immigrants came to the United States in the nineteenth century. Churches and clans were the primary social-service institutions. They wrote letters to loved ones back home for illiterate Chinese men and provided other important community services. Over the years, the Chinese church has resisted assimilation into the greater culture. Members of Chinese churches in the United States and Canada believe in the authority of the Bible; they desire to be separate from secular society; and they wish to live a holy life.

Chinese churches are the fastest-growing churches in Canada; there are at least one hundred in Vancouver. The newest groups of Chinese immigrants are Mandarin-speaking people from Mainland China. Pastor Paul Wang of the Evangelical Christian Bible Church (ECBC), a

Mandarin-speaking Chinese church, says newer immigrants are open to Christianity. When these immigrants come to Canada, they are lonely at first. They have been under a *communist* government that does not recognize God, and they have a spiritual vacuum inside. They have inquisitive minds, however, and often ask many questions about Christianity. When they hear about God's love from Chinese Christians, they are usually spiritually receptive. They are anxious to belong to a group that has a flavor of home and the culture they left behind. The church helps these new immigrants find their place in a new country.

The Chinese Christian Church tends to have active members who follow the Chinese value of placing the good of the group before that of the individual. Pastor Wang says one of their goals is to be honorable citizens of Canada.

Missionaries from Europe and North America initially founded the Christian churches in China and Korea. Centuries later, these churches are returning their own brands of spiritual vitality to the United States and Canada. Other Asian churches have their own ancient history. According to tradition, the *Apostle Thomas* founded the Christian churches in India.

COLOR, CULTURE, CREED, & CHOICES FOR THE FUTURE

In terms of immigrant cultures, the United States and Canada are two of the most diverse nations in the world. Immigrants often come to these nations with spiritual beliefs tied closely to the customs of their homeland. In some cases, the immigrant experience leads people away from their religious practices. However, in just as many cases, immigrants deepen their spiritual beliefs after arriving in North America.

Succeeding generations of immigrants will have to ask, "What is it that makes me Buddhist (or Christian or Hindu or Muslim)?" Many will continue to answer, "My racial (national, tribal, or family) background gives me my religious identity." This answer reflects the importance of group over individual in many non-Western traditions. Others, however, may find themselves agreeing with American evangelist Billy Graham when he says, "God has no grandchildren." They may adopt a more Western, *individualistic* approach to religion. Doing so, they will question, investigate, and choose their own beliefs.

Most citizens of North America do not make religious decisions entirely by background or by individual choice. Religious beliefs are usually a combination of one's heritage and one's individual choices. You may wish to think again about your spiritual background. Where did your ancestors come from? What did they believe? How did their sense of racial, national, and cultural identity influence their religious choices? Finally, how has their cultural and spiritual background influenced you? It can be valuable—even liberating—to understand how your heritage helped create your spiritual beliefs.

FURTHER READING

Balmer, Randall. *Religion in Twentieth Century America.* New York: Oxford University Press, 2001.

Eck, Diana L. *A New Religious America: How a "Christian Country" Has Become the World's Most Religiously Diverse Nation.* New York: Harper San Francisco, 2001.

Elias, Jamal J., adapted by Nancy D. Lewis. *The Pocket Idiot's Guide to Islam.* Indianapolis, Ind.: Alpha Books, 2003.

Klots, Steve. *Indians of North America: Native Americans and Christianity.* Broomall, Pa.: Chelsea House Publishers, 1997.

Lonehill, Karen. *North American Indians Today: Sioux.* Broomall, Pa.: Mason Crest Publishers, 2004.

Lutz, Norma Jean. *The History of the Black Church.* Philadelphia, Pa.: Chelsea House Publishers, 2001.

Maguire, Jack. *Essential Buddhism: A Complete Guide to Beliefs and Practices.* New York: Pocket Books, 2001.

Mann, Gurinder Singh, Paul David Numrich, and Raymond B. Williams. *Religion in American Life: Buddhists, Hindus, and Sikhs in America.* New York: Oxford University Press, 2001.

McIntosh, Kenneth. *North American Indians Today: Navajo.* Broomall, Pa.: Mason Crest Publishers, 2004.

McIntosh, Kenneth. *The Growth of North American Religious Beliefs: Spiritual Diversity.* Broomall, Pa.: Mason Crest Publishers, 2006.

FOR MORE INFORMATION

Asia Information
www.asiasource.org/religion.cfm

Canadian Christianity
www.canadianchristianity.com

Christianity Today
www.christianitytoday.com/ctmag

Goldsea Asian American Supersite
goldsea.com

Hinduism Online
www.himalayanacademy.com

Religious News Service
www.religionnews.com

Religious Tolerance.Org
www.religioustolerance.org/
welcome.htm#new

Sikhe.com
www.sikhe.com

Vietnam in America
mcel.pacificu.edu/as/students/
vietam/aja.html

PICTURE CREDITS

The illustrations in RELIGION AND MODERN CULTURE are photo montages made by Dianne Hodack. They are a combination of her original mixed-media paintings and collages, the photography of Benjamin Stewart, various historical public-domain artwork, and other royalty-free photography collections.

BIOGRAPHIES

AUTHORS: Kenneth and Marsha McIntosh are both former teachers. They have two teen children, Jonathan and Eirene. Marsha has a Bachelor of Science degree in Bible and Education, and Kenneth has a bachelor's degree in English and a master's degree in Theology. Kenneth is an ordained Protestant minister. Marsha tutored Hmong and Mexican American immigrants while working in Minneapolis. She has also worked as administrator for a program serving Central American and Caribbean students in central New York and as a translator for mission service teams in Peru, Honduras, and Guatemala. Kenneth taught in the Los Angeles School System, where the majority of his students were of Mexican or Central American background. Kenneth and Marsha traveled, conducted interviews, and engaged in research for the Mason Crest series NORTH AMERICAN INDIANS TODAY, and Kenneth did the same for the series HISPANIC HERITAGE. They enjoy living in Flagstaff, Arizona, with its rich heritage of American Indian, Latino, and Anglo cultures.

CONSULTANT: Dr. Marcus J. Borg is the Hundere Distinguished Professor of Religion and Culture in the Philosophy Department at Oregon State University. Dr. Borg is past president of the Anglican Association of Biblical Scholars. Internationally known as a biblical and Jesus scholar, the *New York Times* called him "a leading figure among this generation of Jesus scholars." He is the author of twelve books, which have been translated into eight languages. Among them are *The Heart of Christianity: Rediscovering a Life of Faith* (2003) and *Meeting Jesus Again for the First Time* (1994), the best-selling book by a contemporary Jesus scholar.

CONSULTANT: Dr. Robert K. Johnston is Professor of Theology and Culture at Fuller Theological Seminary in Pasadena, California, having served previously as Provost of North Park University and as a faculty member of Western Kentucky University. The author or editor of thirteen books and twenty-five book chapters (including *The Christian at Play*, 1983; *The Variety of American Evangelicalism*, 1991; *Reel Spirituality: Theology and Film in Dialogue*, 2000; *Life Is Not Work/Work Is Not Life: Simple Reminders for Finding Balance in a 24/7 World*, 2000; *Finding God in the Movies: 33 Films of Reel Faith*, 2004; and *Useless Beauty: Ecclesiastes Through the Lens of Contemporary Film*, 2004), Johnston is the immediate past president of the American Theological Society, an ordained Protestant minister, and an avid bodysurfer.